D1404289

A Smart Kid's
Guide to
Personal Finance

How to Make a Budget

Ryan Randolph

PowerKiDS
press

New York

Published in 2014 by The Rosen Publishing Group, Inc.
29 East 21st Street, New York, NY 10010

First Edition

Editor: Jennifer Way
Book Design: Greg Tucker

Photo Credits: Cover, p. 22 Monkey Business Images/Shutterstock.com; pp. 4–5, 8 wavebreakmedia/Shutterstock.com; p. 6 Jupiterimages/Goodshoot/Thinkstock; pp. 7, 10 iStockphoto/Thinkstock; p. 9 Lisa F. Young/Shutterstock.com; p. 11 (top) ZouZou/Shutterstock.com; pp. 11 (bottom), 17 Image Source/Getty Images; p. 12 Vietrov Dmytro/Shutterstock.com; p. 13 (top) Barry Austin Photography/Photodisc/Thinkstock; p. 13 (bottom) mangostock/Shutterstock.com; pp. 14–15 Ariel Skelley/Blend Images/Getty Images; p. 16 Stockbyte/Thinkstock; p. 18 Tyler Olson/Shutterstock.com; p. 19 Digital Vision/Getty Images; pp. 20–21 Huntstock/Thinkstock.

Library of Congress Cataloging-in-Publication Data

Randolph, Ryan P.
 How to make a budget / by Ryan Randolph. — First edition.
     pages cm. — (A smart kid's guide to personal finance)
 Includes index.
 ISBN 978-1-4777-0743-2 (library binding) — ISBN 978-1-4777-0827-9 (pbk.) —
 ISBN 978-1-4777-0828-6 (6-pack)
 1. Budgets, Personal—Juvenile literature. 2. Finance, Personal—Juvenile literature. I. Title.
 HG179.R323628 2014
 332.024—dc23
                        2013000753

Manufactured in the United States of America

CPSIA Compliance Information: Batch #S13PK5: For Further Information contact Rosen Publishing, New York, New York at 1-800-237-9932

Contents

Keeping Track of Money

Have your parents ever said, "We don't have money for that." It is not fun to hear. There are a lot of things to spend money on. People cannot buy everything they want when they want it. How do people figure out what to do with their money? Many people use a helpful spending plan called a **budget**.

A budget is a plan of what and how you will spend the money you earn. Budgeting is a skill that helps you decide what is most important to you and how to pay for it. Adults and businesses use budgets. Kids can use them, too!

4

Budgets help adults pay bills and plan their spending.

5

What Is a Budget?

Businesses budget for expenses such as paying their workers, renting office space, and ordering supplies.

A budget keeps track of the money coming in and the money going out. **Income** can come from gifts, jobs, or an **allowance**. Kids may get allowances for doing chores or simply to give them practice budgeting money. Kids may do extra chores to earn more money.

Money goes out in spending. It could be spent on **expenses**, or things you buy. These can be things you need or things you want, like candy or clothes. Some may be given to **charity**. Money can also be put into savings. A budget helps us decide how and when income is spent.

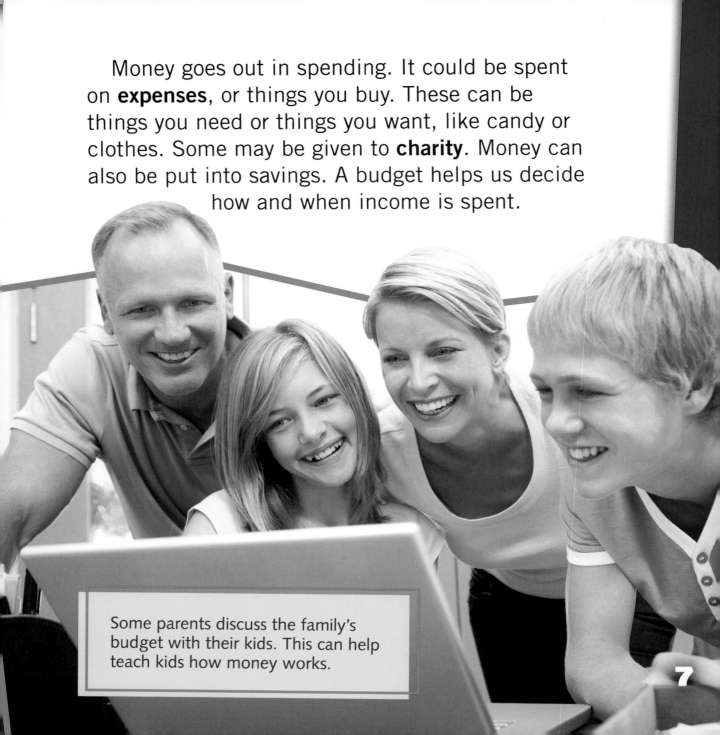

Some parents discuss the family's budget with their kids. This can help teach kids how money works.

Making a Goal

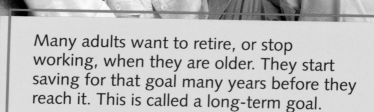

Many adults want to retire, or stop working, when they are older. They start saving for that goal many years before they reach it. This is called a long-term goal.

Have you ever wanted something you did not have enough money for? It might have been a bike, a doll, or a video game. Some kids save for something in the future, like going to college. All of these things are goals.

To reach these goals, saving money is important. This is where budgeting helps. By planning what to spend, you can set aside money to save toward your goal. Budgeting can help you figure out how long it will take you to reach your goal. It can also help you find ways to change your spending **habits** to make reaching your goal easier.

If you want to buy the latest video game, you might save part of your allowance until you have enough money. Buying that game is a short-term goal.

Spending Money

Understanding your expenses, or what you spend money on, is a key part of budgeting. There are different types of expenses. Adults can have expenses for energy, such as gas for the car or oil to heat a house. Kids have expenses, too. The lunch you bought at school is a food expense.

Adults need to budget money to put gas in their cars. They may try to drive less when the price of gas rises so that they do not go over their budgets for this expense.

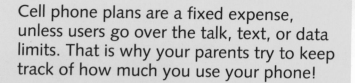

Cell phone plans are a fixed expense, unless users go over the talk, text, or data limits. That is why your parents try to keep track of how much you use your phone!

Some expenses stay the same every month and are things you need every month. These are fixed expenses. Rent on an apartment is a fixed expense. Other expenses are **flexible**, meaning they can change from month to month. Going to the movies and other kinds of entertainment are flexible expenses.

Going to the movies is a flexible expense. People can choose to go to fewer movies when they need to save money.

Things We Need

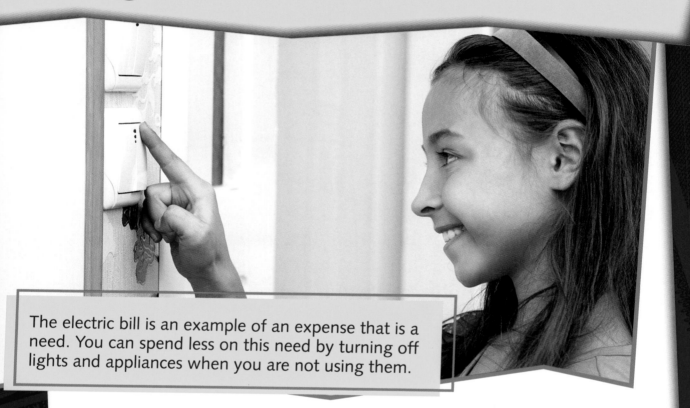

The electric bill is an example of an expense that is a need. You can spend less on this need by turning off lights and appliances when you are not using them.

Listing your monthly expenses is the first step in budgeting. If you want to save more, you will likely need to spend less. How do you decide what to spend less on, though?

Some of the things people spend money on are needs. That means they cannot be cut out of a budget!

Food, clothes, and a place to live are all needs. Some of these things are fixed expenses in a budget. There are ways to spend less on things we need, however. Food is a need, but making dinner at home costs less than eating out at a restaurant, for example.

A big purchase, such as a car, is something many people put money into their savings for before they start shopping for it.

Buying medicine is a need. For most people, it is an expense that changes depending on whether or not they are sick.

Things We Want

Look at your list of monthly expenses again. Did you go to the movies, download a new song, or buy a video game? These expenses are all wants.

Spending less on things you want but do not need allows you to use that money for things that you need. Cutting back on these expenses can help you have more money to save, too. You do not have to cut out your wants entirely, though. You can find cheaper ways to get things you want. You can check books and DVDs out of the library instead of buying them, for example.

Taking dance lessons is a want that is fun and is good exercise. If you wanted to budget less for this, you could find a less expensive place to take lessons.

15

Changing Plans

Sometimes our plans do not work out. Your friend cannot come over because she has too much homework. Plans can be changed. The same thing can happen to your money plans!

If your family adds a new baby, chances are the family's budget will have to change!

Budget changes can happen for a good reason or a bad reason. If someone loses a job, he needs to cut back on his expenses. When someone gets a raise, she might decide to increase her savings or her spending on wants. Goals can change, too. Maybe you were saving for a bike, and you reached that goal and bought it. As your income and goals change, your budget should change, too.

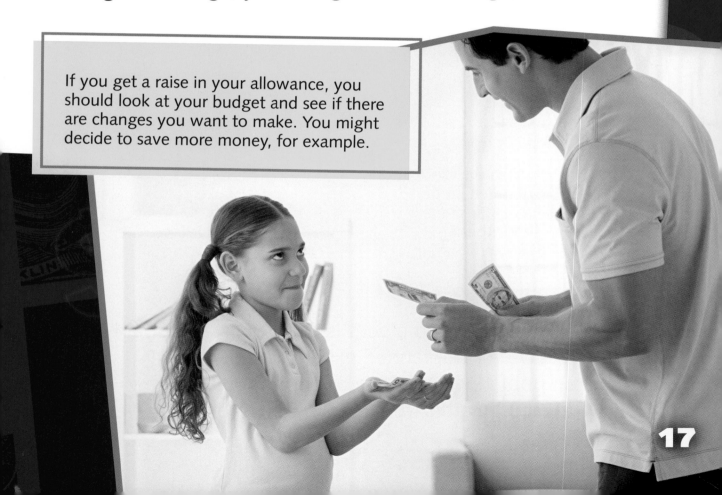

If you get a raise in your allowance, you should look at your budget and see if there are changes you want to make. You might decide to save more money, for example.

Saving Smartly

Unexpected expenses like car repairs can cost a lot of money. Many people start emergency funds so that these expenses do not affect their budgets as badly.

Saving toward a goal is good. It is also smart to save for unplanned expenses. For kids, an unplanned expense might be replacing a friend's toy that you accidentally broke.

People call putting aside savings with no goal "rainy-day" funds or **emergency** funds. Adults need rainy-day funds for things like when the washing machine breaks or the car needs repairs. Being prepared by saving for the unexpected is a smart money move.

An emergency fund is different from the savings used for buying a house. Many people separate their savings into different places to make keeping track of their money easier.

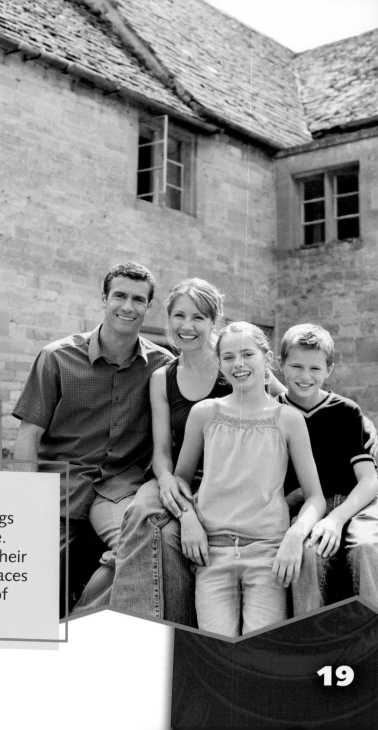

Being Smart About Money

Using a budget to help plan how to spend money is important. Adults use budgeting skills every day. Sometimes things cost more than we have money for. A budget can help us plan how to get these things. It can help us separate needs from wants. By listing expenses, budgets help people decide what is important.

Parents can help guide you in creating a budget, but it is up to you to stick to it. It is not always easy to do this, of course. Forming good budgeting habits early in life is part of developing a skill called **financial responsibility.**

A parent can help you create a budget, and she might also have advice for learning to stick to your budget.

21

Smart Budgeting Tips

1. Record what you spend for one month. Make sure to include the smallest items, from a new pen to a pack of gum. Now you can see where your money goes.

2. Look at your list of expenses. Sort your expenses into wants and needs. Think of ways to cut back your spending on wants. Are there things you can make instead of buying them?

3. Find a safe place to keep your money. Wallets or purses are okay for holding spending money, but a piggy bank or a **savings account** is better for savings.

4. Set up three jars, boxes, or piggy banks. Give them labels such as "spending," "saving," and "giving." When you get money, divide it between the jars according to your budget.

5. When you receive money, put some into your savings first. Think of your savings as "paying yourself first."

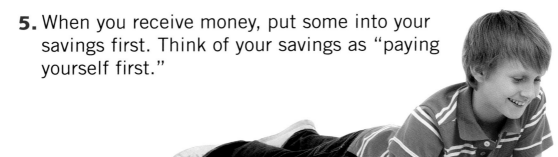

Glossary

allowance (uh-LOW-ents) Money given regularly to someone.

budget (BUH-jit) A plan to spend a certain amount of money in a period of time.

charity (CHER-uh-tee) A group that gives help to the needy.

emergency (ih-MUR-jin-see) An event that happens in which quick help is needed.

expenses (ik-SPENTS-ez) Things on which people spend money.

financial responsibility (fuh-NANT-shul rih-spont-suh-BIH-luh-tee) Using money wisely and well.

flexible (FLEK-sih-bul) Can change.

habits (HA-bits) The ways people or things usually behave.

income (IN-kum) Money received.

savings account (SAYV-ingz uh-KOWNT) A special place where a bank keeps money set aside for someone.

Index

Websites

Due to the changing nature of Internet links, PowerKids Press has developed an online list of websites related to the subject of this book. This site is updated regularly. Please use this link to access the list: www.powerkidslinks.com/skgpf/budget/